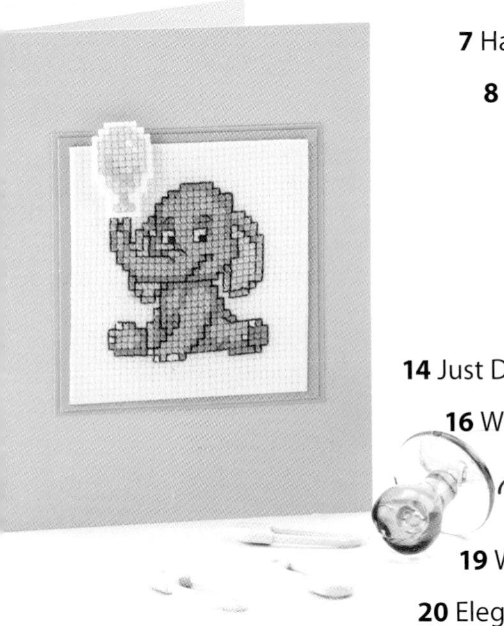

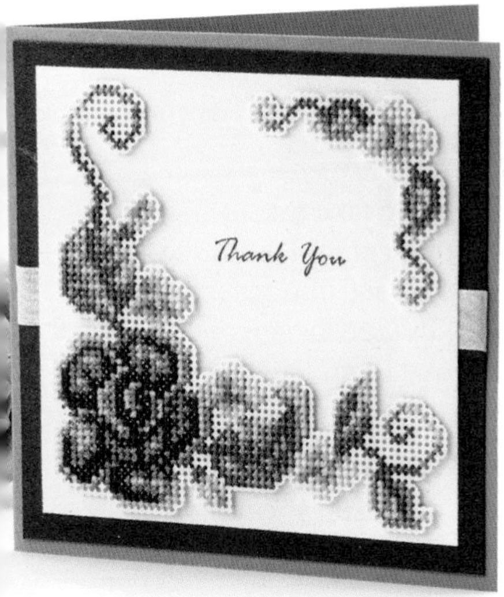

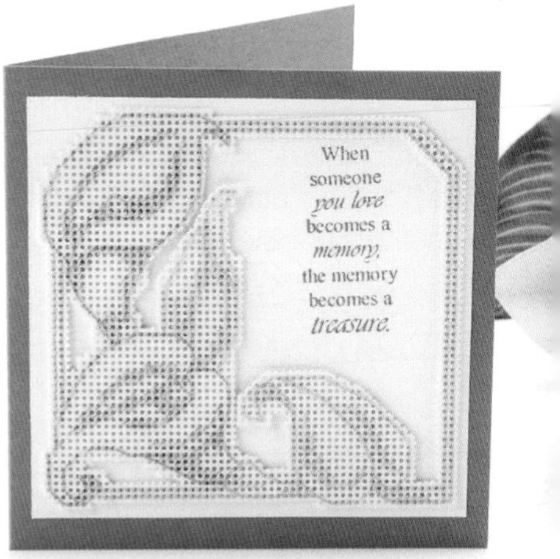

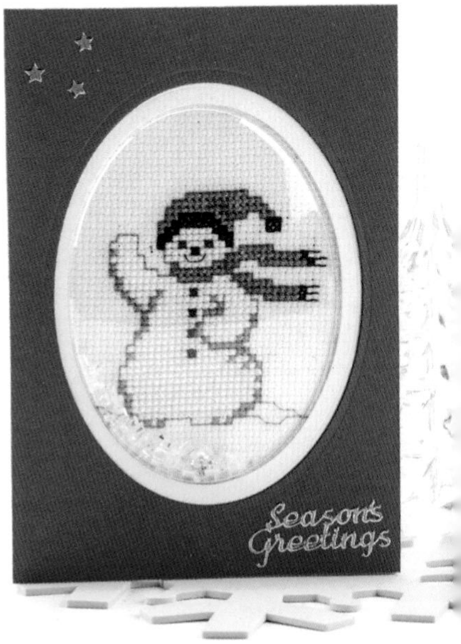

Getting Started

Cross-Stitch Basics

Working From Charted Designs

Each square on a chart corresponds to a space for a cross stitch on the stitching surface. The symbol in a square shows the floss color to be used for the stitch. The width and height for the design stitch area are given; centers are shown by arrows. Backstitches and straight stitches are shown by straight lines, and French knots are shown by dots.

Fabrics & Perforated Paper

The Materials list for each project suggests a working surface that will complement each design. Stitched models were worked on 14-count Aida cloth or on perforated paper, which has 14 squares per inch. On fabrics, the thread count—14-count, 28-count, etc.— refers to the number of threads per inch, and indicates how many cross stitches you can work in 1 inch when stitching over one thread. On 14-count fabric, you can work 14 cross stitches in 1 inch.

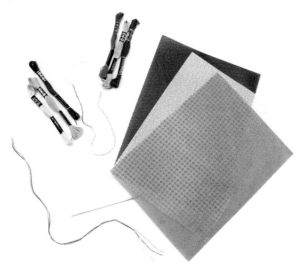

Needles

A blunt-tipped tapestry needle, size 24 or 26, is used for stitching on most 14-count to 28-count fabrics. The higher the needle number, the smaller the needle. The correct-size needle is easy to thread with the amount of floss required, but is not so large that it will distort the holes in the fabric.

Floss

All of our models were stitched using DMC six-strand embroidery floss. Color numbers are given for floss. Cut floss into comfortable working lengths; we suggest about 18 inches. Gently pull apart the strands to separate them, then recombine the number of strands indicated by the pattern (Fig. 1). Do not twist the strands when recombining them for stitching.

Fig. 1

Getting Started

To begin in an unstitched area, bring threaded needle from back to front of fabric (Fig. 2). Hold about ¼ inch of the end of the thread against the back, then anchor it securely in place by catching it under the back loops of your first few stitches (Fig. 3). To end threads and begin new ones next to existing stitches, weave the thread ends through the backs of several stitches.

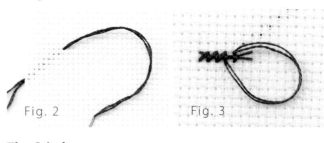

Fig. 2   Fig. 3

The Stitches

The number of strands of floss used for cross stitches will be determined by the thread count of the fabric used and the pattern. Refer to the chart and instructions to determine the number of strands used for cross stitches, backstitches, straight stitches and French knots.

Cross Stitch

A cross stitch is formed in two motions. Follow the numbering in Fig. 4 and bring needle up at 1, down at 2, up at 3 and down at 4 to complete the stitch. Work horizontal rows of stitches wherever possible. Two options exist for stitching. The first option is to bring thread up at 1, work half of each stitch across the row, and then complete the stitches on your return. The second option is to bring thread up at 1 and work each stitch in full before moving on to the next stitch.

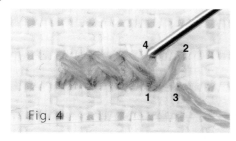
Fig. 4

Half Cross Stitch

For a half cross stitch, work only the bottom layer of a cross stitch (Fig. 5).

Fig. 5

Backstitch

Work backstitches after cross stitches have been completed. They may slope in any direction and are occasionally worked over more than one square of fabric. Fig. 6 shows the progression of several stitches; bring thread up at odd numbers and down at even numbers.

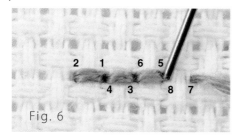
Fig. 6

Straight Stitch

Work straight stitches after cross stitches and backstitches have been completed. They may slope in any direction and are typically worked over more than one square of fabric. Using number of strands indicated in pattern, bring thread up at odd numbers and down at even numbers (Fig. 7).

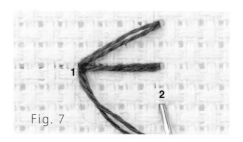
Fig. 7

French Knot

Bring thread up where indicated on chart. Wrap floss once around needle (Fig. 8–10) and reinsert needle into fabric close to the same location. (On fabrics like Jobelan and linen, take the needle back down one thread beyond beginning of stitch; when stitching on Aida cloth, pierce the square near the beginning of the stitch.) Hold the wrapped thread tightly and pull needle through, letting thread go just as knot is formed. Pull gently and firmly, but do not pull too tightly.

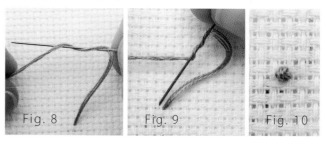
Fig. 8   Fig. 9   Fig. 10

Planning a Project

Before you stitch, decide how large to cut the fabric. Determine the size of the finished stitching, then allow enough additional fabric around the design plus 4–6 inches more on each side for use in finishing and mounting if finishing differently than indicated. Cut your fabric exactly true, right along the holes of the fabric. Some raveling may occur as you handle the fabric. To minimize raveling along the raw edges, use an overcast basting stitch, machine zigzag stitch, or masking tape, which you can cut away when you are finished.

Finishing Needlework

When you have finished stitching, dampen your embroidery (or if soiled, wash in lukewarm mild soapsuds and rinse well). Roll in a towel to remove excess moisture. Place facedown on a dry towel or padded surface; press carefully until dry and smooth. Make sure all thread ends are well anchored and clipped closely. Proceed with instructions for finishing card or tag as given for each design. ❖

Card-Making Basics

Paper

Cardstock is thicker and heavier than regular paper and provides a sturdy surface or base for greeting cards and tags. Most card makers prefer to use at least an 80–100 lb. cardstock for their card bases and lighter-weight varieties for layering.

Cardstock is also available in smooth and textured assortments.

Both options can be used for bases and layering; however, if your design includes stamped images or sentiments, you will want to use a smooth cardstock to get the best image possible.

 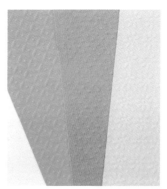

Scoring

A basic scored line is either a depressed or raised line that is created where you want to fold your card. Whether you use a stylus, bone folder or specially created scoring board and tool to create scored lines, the process is virtually the same. Use even pressure and draw the tool down the paper. If you are using a heavy-weight cardstock, you may want to go over the scored line twice.

Scored lines can also be used to create both mountain and valley folds as well as decorative lines to enhance your paper-craft designs.

Die-Cutting

Manual die-cutting machines and die templates make it easy to create special cut shapes directly in your card bases or to use as embellishments. These handy tools eliminate the need for detailed hand cutting and make fast work of creating die-cut pieces. Following the manufacturer's instructions, simply assemble the cutting plates and material that will be cut and run the layered plates through the machine to produce perfectly cut shapes.

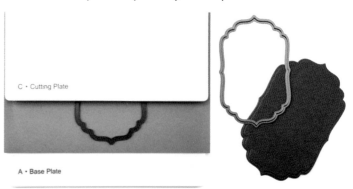

C · Cutting Plate

A · Base Plate

Also available are electronic die-cutting machines like the Provo Craft Cricut® that cut a wide variety of materials, including paper, vinyl, fabric and more. These machines make it easy to create cut shapes using the fonts on your own computer or the designs available from the manufacturer. Improved technology even allows you to create custom-cut shapes.

Adhesives

An extensive variety of adhesive products are available to use for your card and tag projects. Each glue or adhesive is formulated for a particular use and specified surfaces. With all adhesives, read the label and follow the manufacturer's directions for best results.

Dry adhesives are generally the preferred choice with paper crafters; they are easy to apply and require no drying time. The most common types of dry adhesives are double-sided adhesive tabs, tape and tape runners. These products are available in an assortment of sizes and styles. They are often packaged in easy-to-use dispensers, and they can be used on a wide variety of surfaces, including fabric.

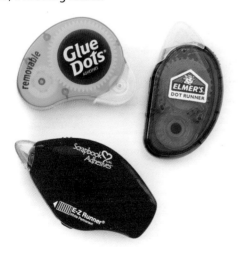

Dimensional adhesives, available as foam tabs and tape and adhesive dots, are another form of dry adhesive that are used to layer elements and create dimension. These products provide a strong hold and can be used with paper and fabric as well as hard embellishments.

Wet adhesives typically offer a strong hold and are often the most economical choice. Wet adhesives are formulated to work best with paper, foam, felt and hard embellishments such as beads and wooden buttons. When applying a wet adhesive to paper, keep in mind that too much wet adhesive may cause your paper to wrinkle or curl. ❖

Birthday

Happy Birthday Tag

Design by **Breanne Jackson**

Materials

- 4 x 6-inch piece Wichelt Imports Inc. 14-count antique brown perforated paper
- 1 skein each DMC 6-strand embroidery floss*
- Size 24 tapestry needle
- Stampin' Up! cardstock: Pacific point, crumb cake
- 3 clear self-adhesive gems
- 12 inches Gina K. Designs ⅜-inch-wide white sheer satin-edge ribbon (optional)
- Spellbinders™ Grand Labels Four die templates (#LF-190)
- Die-cutting machine
- Scoring board and tool
- ⅛-inch hole punch (optional)
- Adhesive

*Refer to color code.

DMC®

■	3834	grape, dk.
@	321	red
♡	603	cranberry
·	726	topaz, lt.
◐	825	blue, dk.
○	906	parrot green, med.

Stitch Count

Happy: 32 x 10
Birthday: 53 x 10

Stitching Size

Happy: 2⅜ x ⅞ inch
Birthday: 3⅞ x ⅞ inch

Tag Size

6 x 3¼ inches

Stitching Instructions

1. Cross stitch over one square using two strands of floss, leaving a margin of at least two unstitched rows between words.

2. Cut stitched designs apart and trim perforated paper to one square from stitching on all sides of each piece.

Tag Assembly

1. Cut a 7 x 8-inch piece of blue cardstock; score and fold in half to create a 7 x 4-inch tag base.

2. Use next-to-smallest Grand Labels Four die template to cut a 6 x 3⅞-inch label-shaped tag from tag base, placing die template beyond fold when cutting to preserve fold.

3. Adhere cross-stitched words to brown cardstock; trim edges even. Adhere words to tag and add gems as shown. *Optional: Punch hole through upper left corner of tag. Loop ribbon through hole; trim ends.* ❖

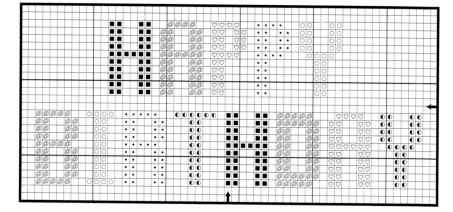

Birthday

Birthday Balloons Shaker Card

Design by **Sharon Pope**

Materials

- 8 x 9-inch piece Wichelt Imports Inc. 14-count white Aida
- 1 skein each DMC 6-strand embroidery floss*
- Size 24 tapestry needle
- Whimsiquills oval domed greeting card blank
- Stampin' Up! melon mambo cardstock
- 3 white self-adhesive pearls
- Gold and silver star confetti
- Spellbinders™ Grand Ovals die templates (#LF-110)
- Die-cutting machine
- Adhesive

*Refer to color code.

DMC®

•	blanc	white
○	350	coral, med.
◐	602	cranberry, med.
♡	603	cranberry
#	725	topaz, med. lt.
~	740	tangerine
⊂	744	yellow, pl.
✳	817	coral red, vy. dk.
■	825	blue, dk.
z	826	blue, med.
★	946	burnt orange, med.
bs	310	black

Stitch Count

54 x 40

Stitching Size

3⅞ x 2⅞ inches

Card Size

5¾ x 4⅛ inches

Stitching Instructions

1. Cross stitch over one square using two strands of floss.

2. Backstitch (bs) over one square using one strand 310.

3. Trim a 5⅛ x 3¾-inch rectangle around stitched image.

Card Assembly

1. Cut a 6 x 4¼-inch piece from pink cardstock.

2. Using smallest Grand Ovals die template, die-cut and emboss a 4¼ x 3¼-inch oval from center of pink rectangle. Adhere rectangle to front of card blank, centering card opening in cutout; trim edges even.

3. Adhere cross-stitched balloons to inside of card panel that will show through to card front.

4. Apply adhesive on front edges of clear dome; adhere to reverse side of card front, covering oval opening.

5. Fill clear dome with confetti as desired. Apply adhesive along edges of dome and close card, sealing dome closed.

6. Attach pearls to lower right corner of card front as shown. ❖

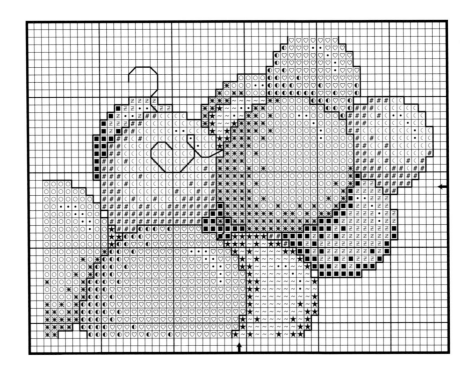

Celebrate!

Design by **Elizabeth Spurlock**

Materials
- 9 x 9-inch piece Wichelt Imports Inc. 14-count white Aida
- 1 skein each DMC 6-strand embroidery floss*
- Size 24 tapestry needle
- Stampin' Up! cardstock: daffodil delight, rich razzleberry, melon mambo
- Sentiment stamp
- Purple ink pad
- 12 inches Gina K. Designs ⅜-inch-wide sheer pink ribbon
- Scoring board and tool
- Adhesives: paper adhesive, adhesive foam tape

*Refer to color code.

DMC®

╱	518	Wedgwood, lt.
◖	602	cranberry, med.
@	603	cranberry
♡	605	cranberry, vy. lt.
·	726	topaz, lt.
■	3834	grape, dk.
X	3835	grape, med.

Stitch Count
43 x 54

Stitching Size
3⅛ x 3⅞ inches

Card Size
4¼ x 5½ inches

Stitching Instructions

1. Cross stitch over one square using two strands of floss.

2. Trim fabric to one square from stitching on all edges.

Card Assembly

1. Cut a 4¼ x 11-inch piece from melon cardstock; score and fold in half to create a 4¼ x 5½-inch card.

2. Cut a 3¾ x 5⅛-inch piece from yellow cardstock; using foam tape, center and adhere yellow cardstock to a 4⅛ x 5⅜-inch piece of berry cardstock. Center and adhere layered panel to card front.

3. Wrap ribbon around cupcake and tie ends in a bow; trim ribbon ends. Adhere cupcake to card front as shown.

4. Stamp desired sentiment onto card front below cupcake. ❖

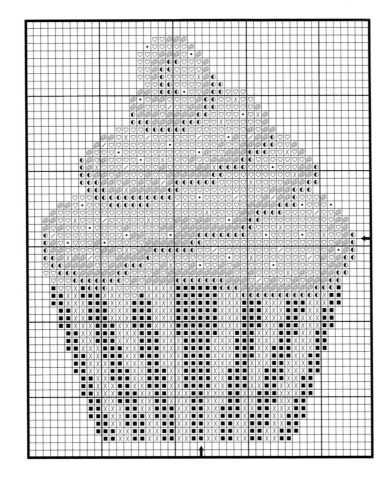

Baby

BABY Gift Tag

Design by **Breanne Jackson**

Materials
- 5 x 8-inch piece Wichelt Imports Inc. 14-count white perforated paper
- 1 skein each DMC 6-strand embroidery floss*
- Size 24 tapestry needle
- Stampin' Up! cardstock: whisper white, blushing bride
- 9 inches Gina K. Designs ⅜-inch-wide pink stitched ribbon
- ⅛-inch hole punch
- Adhesive

*Refer to color code.

DMC®
◇ 368   pistachio green, lt.
• 745   pale yellow, lt.
♡ 963   dusty rose, ul. vy. lt.
○ 3841 baby blue, pl.

Stitch Count
13 x 13 each (4)

Stitching Size
1 x 1 inch each

Tag Size
5½ x 1½ inches

Stitching Instructions

1. Cross stitch over one square using two strands of floss, leaving at least two unstitched rows between blocks.

2. Cut out each block and trim perforated paper to one square from stitching on all sides of each piece.

Tag Assembly

1. Cut a 5½ x 1½-inch rectangle from pink cardstock for tag base. Use scissors to round off corners on right end of tag as shown.

2. Adhere cross-stitched letter blocks to white cardstock; trim edges even. Adhere blocks to tag as shown.

3. Punch a hole in right end of tag; loop ribbon through hole and trim ends. ❖

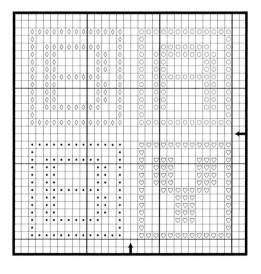

Baby

Just Ducky Rocker Card

Design by **Sharon Pope**

Materials

- 5 x 8-inch piece Wichelt Imports Inc. 14-count white perforated paper
- 1 skein each DMC 6-strand embroidery floss*
- Size 24 tapestry needle
- Stampin' Up! cardstock: midnight muse, marina mist, soft sky
- Sticky notes
- Spellbinders™ die templates: Grand Circles (#LF-114), Classic Scallop (#E8-001)
- Die-cutting machine
- Scoring board and tool
- Elmer's adhesive runner

*Refer to color code.

DMC®

•	blanc	white
■	310	black
X	740	tangerine
@	743	yellow, med.
○	744	yellow, pl.
~	745	yellow, pl. lt.
★	946	burnt orange, med.
μ	3854	autumn gold, med.

Stitch Count

42 x 40

Stitching Size

3 x 2⅞ inches

Card Size

5¾ x 4¼ inches

Stitching Instructions

1. Cross stitch over one square using two strands of floss.

2. Backstitch over one square using one strand 310.

3. Trim perforated paper to one square from stitching on all sides.

Card Assembly

1. Using Grand Circles die template, die-cut a 5¾-inch circle from light blue cardstock. Score and fold in half to create card base (Photo 1).

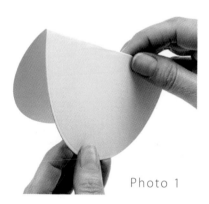

Photo 1

2. Cut two 6 x 1-inch strips from each blue cardstock for a total of six strips. Using the Classic Scallops die template, die-cut and emboss scalloped "waves" from blue strips (Photo 2).

Photo 2

3. Working on Cutting Plate, position waves as desired and place Grand Circles die template over layered waves. Use sticky notes to hold pieces in place and die-cut to fit card front. (Photo 3).

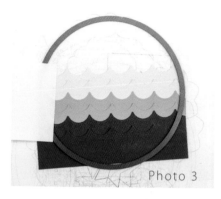

Photo 3

4. Apply adhesive around bottom edge only of each die-cut wave; adhere waves to card base as shown, starting at card top and working down (Photo 4).

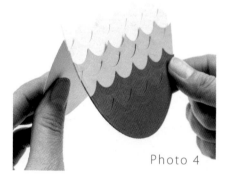

Photo 4

5. Insert and adhere cross-stitched ducky between waves as shown. ❖

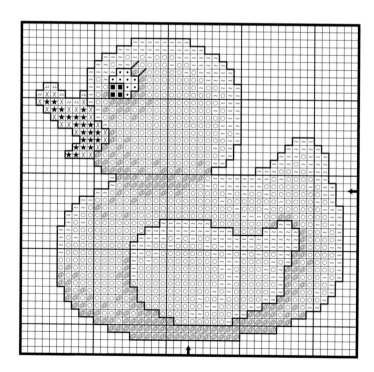

Welcome Little One

Design by **Angela Pullen Atherton**

Materials

- 5 x 8-inch piece Wichelt Imports Inc. 14-count white Aida
- 1 skein each DMC 6-strand embroidery floss*
- Size 24 tapestry needle
- Stampin' Up! cardstock: so saffron, whisper white, blushing bride, pear pizzazz
- Scoring board and tool
- Adhesives: adhesive foam squares, adhesive runner

*Refer to color code.

DMC®

•	blanc	white
◑	318	steel gray, lt.
■	413	pewter gray, dk.
X	415	pearl gray
@	743	yellow, med.
~	744	yellow, pl.
♡	963	dusty rose, ul. vy. lt.

Stitch Count

Elephant: 25 x 27
Balloon: 7 x 13

Stitching Size

Elephant: 1¾ x 2 inches
Balloon: ½ x 1 inch

Card Size

4½ x 5½ inches

Stitching Instructions

1. Cross stitch over one square using two strands of floss.

2. Backstitch (bs) over one square using one strand 743 for balloon and 413 for elephant.

3. Cut out balloon, trimming fabric to one square from stitching along all edges. Cut a rectangle around elephant, trimming fabric to six squares from the widest point of stitching on each side.

Card Assembly

1. Cut an 8½ x 5½-inch piece from yellow cardstock; score and fold in half to create a 4¼ x 5½-inch card.

2. Adhere cross-stitched elephant to white cardstock; trim edges even.

3. Adhere elephant panel to pink cardstock and trim, leaving a narrow border. Adhere panel to green cardstock and trim, leaving a very narrow border. Adhere elephant panel to card front as shown.

4. Stack two foam squares; attach to reverse side of cross-stitched balloon and attach to card front as shown. ❖

Wedding

Wedding Cake Tag

Design by **Elizabeth Spurlock**

Materials

- 5 x 5-inch piece Wichelt Imports Inc. 14-count antique brown perforated paper
- 1 skein each DMC 6-strand embroidery floss*
- Size 24 tapestry needle
- Stampin' Up! wild wasabi cardstock
- 15 inches Gina K. Designs ⅜-inch-wide grass green organza ribbon
- Spellbinders™ Labels Four die templates (#S4-190)
- Die-cutting machine
- ⅛-inch hole punch
- Adhesive

*Refer to color code.

DMC®

•	blanc	white
■	351	coral
♡	352	coral, lt.
@	368	pistachio green, lt.
X	598	turquoise, lt.

Stitch Count

33 x 42

Stitching Size

2⅜ x 3 inches

Tag Size

2¾ x 4⅜ inches

Stitching Instructions

1. Cross stitch over one square using two strands of floss.

2. Trim perforated paper to one square from stitching along all edges.

Tag Assembly

1. Use the largest of the Labels Four die templates to die-cut and emboss a 2¾ x 4⅜-inch shape from cardstock.

2. Adhere cross-stitched wedding cake to tag as shown.

3. Punch a hole near top of tag; loop ribbon through hole and V-notch ribbon ends. ❖

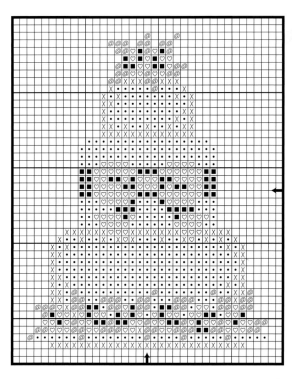

Elegant Gatefold Card

Design by **Angela Pullen Atherton**

Materials
- 5 x 8-inch piece Wichelt Imports Inc. 14-count white perforated paper
- 1 skein each DMC 6-strand embroidery floss*
- Size 24 tapestry needle
- 12 x 12-inch sheet aqua cardstock
- 20 inches Gina K. Designs ⅜-inch-wide green sheer ribbon
- Scoring board and tool
- ⅛-inch hole punch
- Adhesive foam tape

*Refer to color code.

DMC®

•	blanc	white
~	162	blue, ul. vy. lt.
ℓ	164	forest green, lt.
z	209	lavender, dk.
◑	347	salmon, vy. dk.
☆	725	topaz, med. lt.
Ʒ	813	blue, lt.
○	827	blue, vy. lt.
■	986	forest green, vy. dk.
@	988	forest green, med.
♡	3712	salmon, med.
∕	3713	salmon, vy. lt.

Stitch Count
26 x 70 each (2)

Stitching Size
1⅞ x 5 inches each (2)

Card Size
4 x 5¼ inches

Stitching Instructions

1. Cross stitch motifs over one square using two strands of floss, leaving a margin of at least two unstitched rows between motifs.

2. Backstitch over one square using one strand 813.

3. Cut out stitched images, trimming perforated paper to one square from stitching along all edges of each piece.

Card Assembly

1. Cut a 12 x 5¼-inch piece from cardstock.

2. Place cardstock on scoring board with long edges horizontal. Using scoring tool, score cardstock vertically at 2-inch, 4-inch, 8-inch and 10-inch marks (Photo 1).

Photo 1

3. Accordion-fold side panels inward (Photo 2).

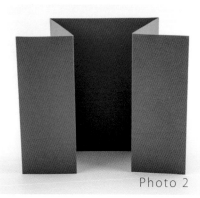

Photo 2

4. With side panels folded in on one side, punch a hole through front and second panels near fold and 3 inches from bottom (Photo 3). Punch a matching hole through folded panels on other side.

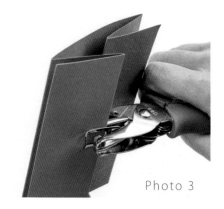

Photo 3

5. Cut two 10-inch pieces of ribbon. Thread one piece through each pair of holes, knotting ribbon on reverse side (Photo 4).

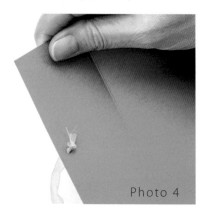

Photo 4

6. Attach cross-stitched motifs to card front as shown. Tie card shut with ribbon; V-notch ribbon ends. ❖

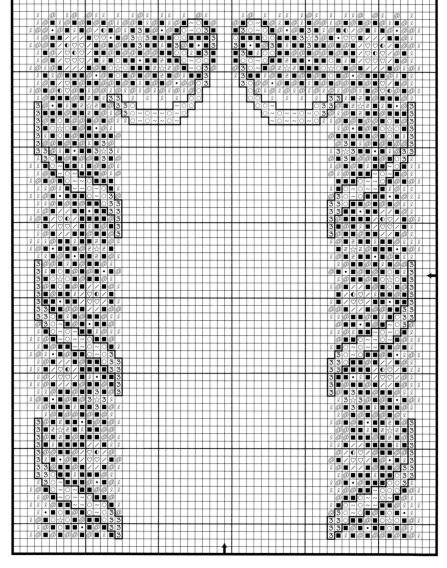

Wedding

For the Love Birds

Design by **Breanne Jackson**

Materials
- 5 x 8-inch piece Wichelt Imports Inc. 14-count white perforated paper
- 1 skein each DMC 6-strand embroidery floss*
- Size 24 tapestry needle
- Stampin' Up! cardstock: whisper white, calypso coral, wild wasabi
- Sticky notes
- Spellbinders™ Classic Petal die templates (#E8-006)
- Die-cutting machine
- Scoring board and tool
- Adhesive: adhesive foam tape, adhesive tape runner

*Refer to color code.

DMC®
♥	350	coral, med.
○	368	pistachio green, lt.
@	414	steel gray, dk.
•	762	pearl gray, vy. lt.

Stitch Count
Dove: 16 x 17 each (2)
Heart: 11 x 11

Stitching Size
Dove: 1¼ x 1¼ inches each (2)
Heart: ⅞ x ⅞ inch

Card Size
5½ x 3⅜ inches

Stitching Instructions
1. Cross stitch over one square using two strands of floss, leaving at least two unstitched rows between motifs.

2. Backstitch over one square using one strand 414. Work French knots where • appears using one strand 414 and wrapping floss around needle twice.

3. Cut out each motif and trim perforated paper to one square from stitching on all edges of each piece.

Card Assembly

1. Cut a 5½ x 6¾-inch piece from green cardstock; score and fold in half to create a 5½ x 3⅜-inch card base.

2. Cut a 5½ x 1¾-inch piece from white cardstock. Using foam tape, attach doves and heart as shown in photo.

3. Cut a 5½ x 6½-inch piece from coral cardstock. Using Edger die template with Hearts and Circles insert, die-cut and emboss along one short edge as shown (Photo 1). *Note: Use sticky notes to secure the die templates in place.*

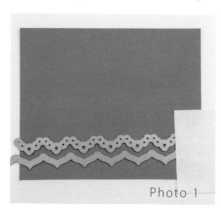

Photo 1

4. Score and fold die-cut cardstock 3 inches from die-cut edge. Adhere to card base as shown, folding excess over top edge of card and adhering to back.

5. Adhere white panel with cross-stitched motifs to card front as shown. ❖

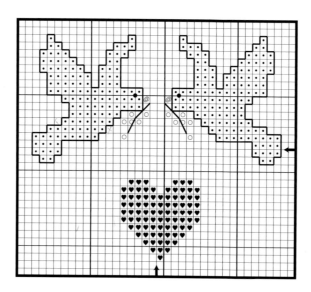

Thank You

Thank You

Thank You Tag

Design by **Christy Schmitz**

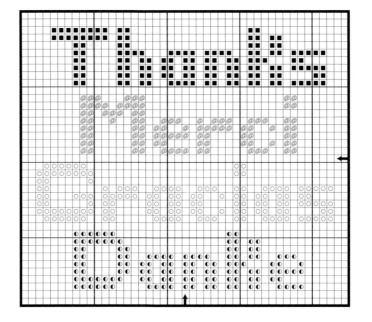

Materials
- 5 x 5-inch piece Wichelt Imports Inc. 14-count antique brown perforated paper
- 1 skein each DMC 6-strand embroidery floss*
- Size 24 tapestry needle
- Stampin' Up! cardstock: tempting turquoise, Pacific point, crumb cake
- We R Memory Keepers metallic floss: 9 inches blue, 9 inches gold
- ⅛-inch hole punch
- Adhesive

*Refer to color code.

DMC®
◑	3761	sky blue, lt.
■	3844	bright turquoise, dk.
@	3845	bright turquoise, med.
○	3846	bright turquoise, lt.

Stitch Count
41 x 35

Stitching Size
2⅞ x 2½ inches

Tag Size
4 x 3½ inches

Stitching Instructions
1. Cross stitch over one square using two strands of floss.

2. Cut a rectangle around design as shown, trimming perforated paper to one square from widest point of stitching on each side.

Tag Assembly
1. Cut a 4 x 3½-inch piece from dark blue cardstock for tag base.

2. Adhere cross-stitched piece to brown cardstock and trim a narrow border; adhere panel to turquoise cardstock and trim a narrow border. Center and adhere layered panel to tag base.

3. Punch a hole through upper left corner of tag; loop blue and gold floss through hole. ❖

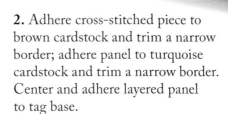

Thank You

Thank You Card

Design by **Angela Pullen Atherton**

Materials
- 6 x 6-inch piece Wichelt Imports Inc. 14-count white perforated paper
- 1 skein each DMC 6-strand embroidery floss*
- Size 24 tapestry needle
- Stampin' Up! cardstock: very vanilla, melon mambo, old olive
- Gina K. Designs Wild at Heart stamp set
- Stampin' Up! not quite navy ink pad
- 6 inches Gina K. Designs ½-inch-wide white satin ribbon
- Scoring board and tool
- Adhesive

*Refer to color code.

DMC®

■	469	avocado green
@	470	avocado green, lt.
╱	472	avocado green, ul. lt.
♥	601	cranberry, dk.
○	603	cranberry
·	605	cranberry, vy. lt.
★	721	orange spice, med.
μ	743	yellow, med.
~	828	blue, ul. vy. lt.
#	3844	bright turquoise, dk.
☆	3846	bright turquoise, lt.

Stitch Count
Large motif: 56 x 56
Small motif: 26 x 26

Stitching Size
Large motif: 4 x 4 inches
Small motif: 1⅞ x 1⅞ inches

Card Size
5 x 5 inches

Stitching Instructions

1. Cross stitch over one square using two strands of floss.

2. Backstitch over one square using one strand 601 for rose, 469 for green leaves, and 3844 for blue flowers.

3. Cut apart motifs, trimming perforated paper to one square from stitching along all edges of each piece.

Card Assembly

1. Cut a 5 x 10-inch piece from green cardstock; score and fold in half to create a 5 x 5-inch card.

2. Cut a 4¼ x 4¼-inch piece from ivory cardstock. Adhere cross-stitched motifs to cardstock as shown; stamp sentiment on cardstock.

3. Cut a 4¾ x 4¾-inch piece from melon cardstock. Wrap ribbon around center of cardstock as shown; adhere ends on reverse side.

4. Center and adhere cross-stitched panel to melon panel; center and adhere layered panels to card front. ❖

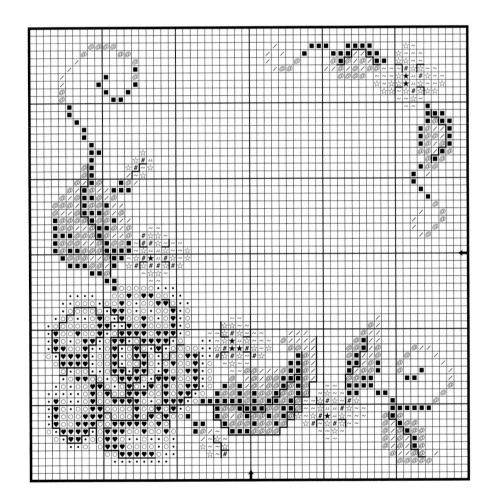

Thank You So Much

Design by **Breanne Jackson**

Materials

- 7 x 10-inch piece Wichelt Imports Inc. 14-count black Aida
- 1 skein DMC 6-strand embroidery floss*
- Size 24 tapestry needle
- Stampin' Up! basic black cardstock
- Scoring board and tool
- Adhesive

*Refer to color code.

DMC®

- blanc   white

Stitch Count
59 x 41

Stitching Size
4⅜ x 3⅛ inches

Card Size
5½ x 4¼ inches

Stitching Instructions

1. Cross stitch over one square using two strands of floss.

2. Backstitch over one square using two strands of floss.

3. Cut a rectangle around design, trimming fabric to two squares from stitched border.

Card Assembly

1. Cut a 5½ x 8½-inch piece from cardstock; score and fold in half to create a 5½ x 4¼-inch card base.

2. Center and adhere cross-stitched design to a 4⅝ x 3¼-inch piece of cardstock. Center and adhere cross-stitched panel to card front as shown. ❖

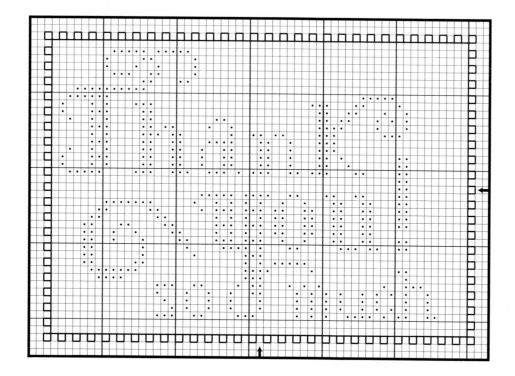

Thinking of You

When someone *you love* becomes a *memory*, the memory becomes a *treasure*.

Forget-Me-Not Tag

Design by **Angela Pullen Atherton**

Materials
- 5 x 4-inch piece Wichelt Imports Inc. 14-count antique brown perforated paper
- 1 skein each DMC 6-strand embroidery floss*
- Size 24 tapestry needle
- Stampin' Up! so saffron cardstock
- Ranger white opal Liquid Pearls
- 11 inches Gina K. Designs ⅜-inch-wide ivory satin ribbon
- Spellbinders™ Grand Ovals die templates (#LF-110)
- Die-cutting machine
- ⅛-inch hole punch
- Scoring board and tool
- Adhesive

*Refer to color code.

DMC®
■	322	baby blue, vy. dk.
★	580	moss green, dk.
X	581	moss green
☆	726	topaz, lt.
3	728	topaz
•	775	baby blue, vy. lt.
~	3078	golden yellow, vy. lt.
♡	3325	baby blue, lt.
@	3755	baby blue
bs	3828	hazelnut brown

Stitch Count
42 x 36

Stitching Size
3 x 2⅝ inches

Tag Size
4⅛ x 3¼ inches

Stitching Instructions
1. Cross stitch over one square using two strands of floss.

2. Backstitch (bs) over one square using one strand 3828.

3. Trim perforated paper to one square from stitching along all edges.

Tag Assembly
1. Cut an 11 x 4¼-inch piece from cardstock; score and fold in half to form a 5½ x 4¼-inch tag.

2. Use smallest Grand Ovals die template to die-cut and emboss a 4¼ x 3¼-inch oval from tag, positioning die template beyond fold to create oval tag.

3. Adhere cross-stitched motif to tag. Add a border of Liquid Pearls dots around edges; let dry.

4. Punch a hole in the upper left edge of tag; loop ribbon through hole and trim ends. ❖

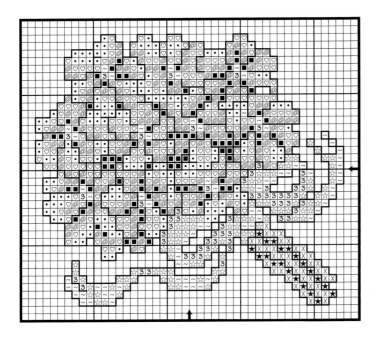

Thinking of You

Get Well Easel Card

Design by **Sharon Pope**

Materials
- 9 x 9-inch piece Wichelt Imports Inc. 14-count white Aida
- 1 skein each DMC 6-strand embroidery floss*
- Size 24 tapestry needle
- Stampin' Up! cardstock: whisper white, calypso coral, wisteria wonder
- 5 inches Stampin' Up! ⅝-inch-wide Crochet Trim Victoria ribbon
- My Favorite Things yellow buttons: 1 large, 2 small
- Scoring board and tool
- Adhesive

*Refer to color code.

DMC®

~	164	forest green, lt.
■	310	black
☆	340	blue violet, med.
╱	341	blue violet, lt.
◑	351	coral
@	352	coral, lt.
·	353	peach
3	676	old gold, lt.
X	989	forest green

Stitch Count
55 x 55

Stitching Size
4 x 4 inches

Card Size
5 x 5 inches

Stitching Instructions

1. Cross stitch over one square using two strands of floss.

2. Backstitch over one square using one strand 310.

3. Trim stitched design to approximately 4¼ x 4¼ inches, trimming fabric to two squares from widest point of stitching on each side.

Card Assembly

1. Cut a 5 x 10-inch piece from lavender cardstock. Place cardstock on scoring board with long edge horizontal and use scoring tool to score vertical lines at 5-inch and 7½-inch marks (Photo 1). Fold at 5-inch scored line to create card base; fold downward at 7½-inch scored line to create easel front (Photo 2). Set aside.

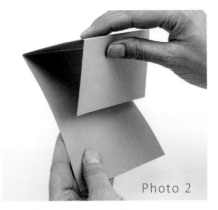

Photo 2

Photo 3

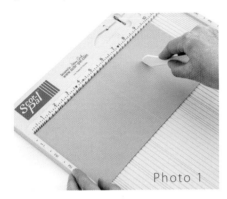

Photo 1

2. Adhere cross-stitched piece to white cardstock; trim edges even. Adhere to coral cardstock; trim, leaving a narrow border. Center and adhere panel to a 5 x 5-inch piece of lavender cardstock. Adhere piece to card front, adhering bottom half only (Photo 3).

3. Open card and adhere crochet trim inside card 1 inch from bottom edge. Center and adhere buttons to crochet trim as shown. The card front can be folded up to form an easel, and the buttons will hold card front in place. ❖

Thinking of You

Lilies Sympathy Card

Design by **Elizabeth Spurlock**

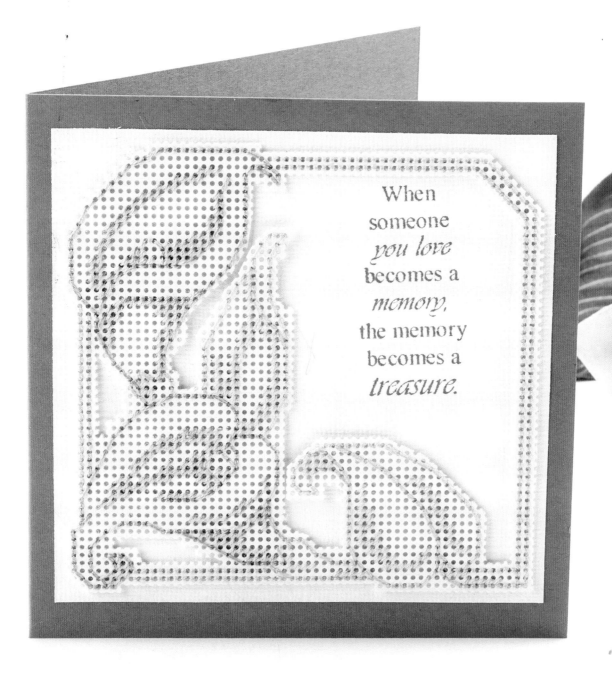

When someone *you love* becomes a *memory,* the memory becomes a *treasure.*

Materials

- 7 x 7-inch piece Wichelt Imports Inc. 14-count white perforated paper
- 1 skein each DMC 6-strand embroidery floss*
- Size 24 tapestry needle
- Stampin' Up! cardstock: wild wasabi, whisper white
- Gina K. Designs A Beautiful Life stamp set
- Stampin' Up! old olive ink pad
- Scoring board and tool
- Adhesive

*Refer to color code.

DMC®

@	164	forest green, lt.
╱	341	blue violet, lt.
○	676	old gold, lt.

Stitch Count

56 x 54

Stitching Size

4 x 3⅞ inches

Card Size

4¾ x 4¾ inches

Stitching Instructions

1. Work half cross stitch over one square using two strands of floss.

2. Backstitch over one square using two strands 164 for leaves and stems, 341 for flowers, and 676 for stamens and border.

3. Trim perforated paper to one square from stitching along all edges outside *and* inside design.

Card Assembly

1. Cut a 9½ x 4¾-inch piece from green cardstock; score and fold in half to form a 4¾ x 4¾-inch card.

2. Cut a 4¼ x 4⅛-inch piece from white cardstock. Adhere cross-stitched motif to cardstock; center and adhere to card front.

3. Stamp sentiment onto card front as shown. ❖

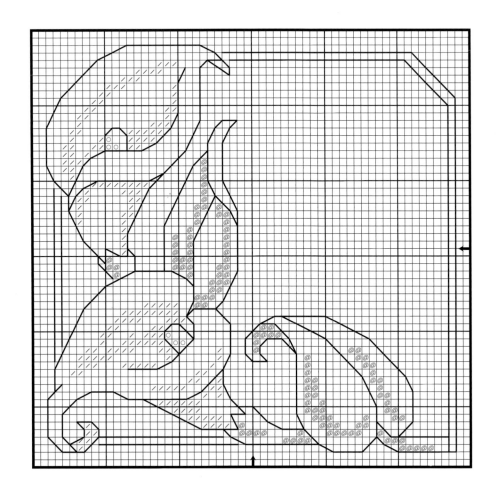

Halloween

Candy Corn Tag

Design by **Christy Schmitz**

Materials

- 10 x 6-inch piece Wichelt Imports Inc. 14-count antique brown perforated paper
- 1 skein each DMC 6-strand embroidery floss*
- Size 24 tapestry needle
- Stampin' Up! cardstock: crumb cake, crushed curry, whisper white, pumpkin pie
- 9 inches We R Memory Keepers brown baker's twine
- ⅛-inch hole punch
- Adhesive

*Refer to color code.

DMC®

- blanc — white
- ○ 743 — yellow, med.
- ■ 947 — burnt orange

Stitch Count

35 x 42

Stitching Size

3⅛ x 2⅜ inches

Tag Size

3¾ x 4⅛ inches

Stitching Instructions

1. Cross stitch over one square using two strands of floss.

2. Trim perforated paper to one square from stitching on all sides.

Tag Assembly

1. Adhere cross-stitched candy corn to brown cardstock; trim edges even.

2. Adhere candy corn to yellow cardstock and trim a narrow border. Adhere to white cardstock and trim a very narrow border. Adhere to orange cardstock and trim a wide border as shown.

3. Punch a hole through center top of tag; loop baker's twine through hole and trim ends. ❖

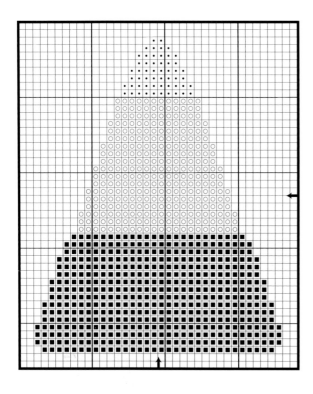

Halloween

Boo! Swing Card

Design by **Elizabeth Spurlock**

Materials
- 10 x 6-inch piece Wichelt Imports Inc. 14-count white perforated paper
- 1 skein each DMC 6-strand embroidery floss*
- Size 24 tapestry needle
- Stampin' Up! cardstock: old olive, pumpkin pie, early espresso
- 5½ inches Stampin' Up! early espresso ¼-inch-wide stitched grosgrain ribbon
- Scoring board and tool
- Craft knife
- Cutting mat
- Elmer's paper adhesive

*Refer to color code.

DMC®
◑	300	mahogany, vy. dk.
X	434	brown, lt.
@	552	violet, med.
•	739	tan, ul. vy. lt.
╱	745	yellow, pl. lt.
#	898	coffee brown, vy. dk.
~	907	parrot green, lt.
■	3371	black brown
☆	3853	autumn gold, dk.

Stitch Count
Owls: 41 x 42 each (2)
Boo: 12 x 42

Stitching Size
Owls: 2⅞ x 3 inches each
Boo: ⅞ x 3 inches

Card Size
4¼ x 5½ inches

Stitching Instructions
1. Cross stitch motifs over one square using two strands of floss, leaving a margin of at least two unstitched rows between motifs.

2. Cut out stitched images, trimming perforated paper to one square from stitching along all edges of each piece.

Card Assembly
1. Cut a 6⅜ x 5½-inch piece from green cardstock for card base.

2. Place cardstock on scoring board with long edges horizontal. Using scoring tool, score cardstock vertically 2¾ inches and 4 inches from left edge (Photo 1).

Photo 1

3. Using a pencil, lightly outline a rectangle 1 inch from top and bottom edges and 1¼ inches from left and right edges (Photo 2).

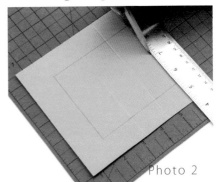
Photo 2

4. Place cardstock on cutting mat. Using a craft knife, carefully cut lines on left and right edges; cut along top and bottom lines, stopping at scored lines (Photo 3).

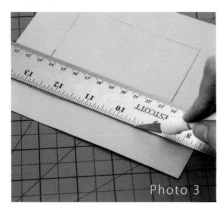

Photo 3

5. Fold card panels in opposite directions along scored lines to create a swinging panel (Photo 4).

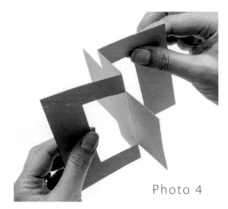

Photo 4

6. Cut a ¾ x 5½-inch strip from orange cardstock; adhere to front panel of card along left edge as shown. Center and adhere ribbon to strip as shown.

7. Cut two 3⅞ x 3⅜-inch pieces from orange cardstock; adhere to front and back of swinging panel. Adhere cross-stitched owls to orange cardstock panels and "BOO!" to card as shown. ❖

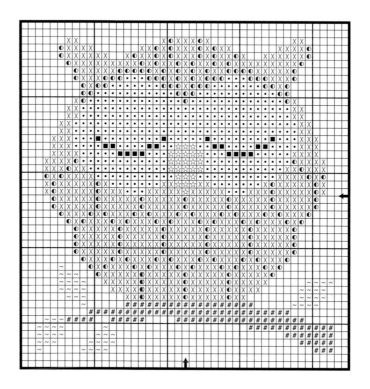

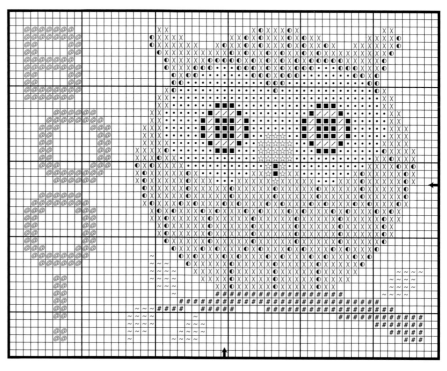

Hey Punkin!

Design by **Angela Pullen Atherton**

Materials
- 9 x 10-inch piece Wichelt Imports Inc. 14-count black Aida
- 1 skein each DMC 6-strand embroidery floss*
- Size 24 tapestry needle
- Stampin' Up! cardstock: basic black, pear pizzazz, perfect plum
- Scoring board and tool
- Adhesive

*Refer to color code.

DMC®

⁄	166	moss green, med. lt.
~	209	lavender, dk.
■	327	violet, dk.
@	580	moss green, dk.
○	581	moss green
•	745	yellow, pl. lt.
X	946	burnt orange, med.
★	970	pumpkin, lt.
☆	3837	lavender, ul. dk.
bs	301	mahogany, med.

Stitch Count
63 x 45

Stitching Size
4⅝ x 3⅜ inches

Card Size
5½ x 4¼ inches

Stitching Instructions

1. Cross stitch over one square using two strands of floss.

2. Backstitch (bs) over one square using one strand 301 for pumpkin sections and 580 for vines, tendrils and leaves.

3. Cut a rectangle around design as shown, trimming Aida to two squares from outermost edge of design on each side.

Card Assembly

1. Cut a 5½ x 8½-inch piece from purple cardstock; score and fold in half to create a 5½ x 4¼-inch card.

2. Adhere cross-stitched panel to black cardstock; trim edges even.

3. Adhere panel to green cardstock and trim, leaving a very narrow border. Center and adhere layered panel to card front. ***Note:*** *If desired, replace wording with personalized message using alphabet on page 41.* ❖

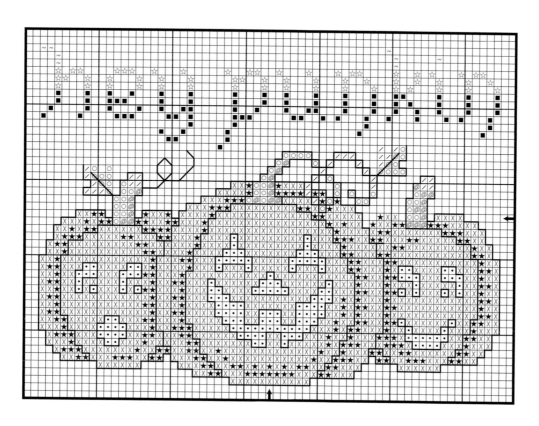

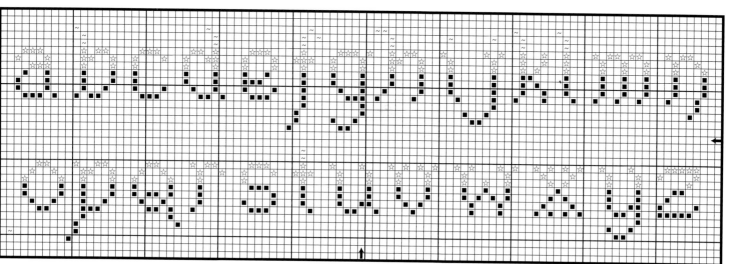

Christmas

Holiday Ornaments Gift Tag

Design by **Breanne Jackson**

Materials
- 5 x 5-inch piece Wichelt Imports Inc. 14-count antique brown perforated paper
- 1 skein each DMC 6-strand embroidery floss*
- Size 24 tapestry needle
- Stampin' Up! pear pizzazz cardstock
- Black fine-tip pen
- 9 inches Gina K. Designs ⅜-inch-wide olive green sheer ribbon
- ⅛-inch hole punch
- Adhesive

*Refer to color code.

DMC®

◑	321	red
◊	471	avocado green, vy. lt.
@	937	avocado green, med.
#	3766	peacock blue, lt.
■	3799	pewter gray, vy. dk.
ss	712	cream

Stitch Count
31 x 38

Stitching Size
2¼ x 2¾ inches

Tag Size
6 x 3 inches

Stitching Instructions

1. Cross stitch over one square using two strands of floss.

2. Backstitch over one square using one strand 3799.

3. Work straight stitches (ss) over cross stitches using one strand 712.

4. Trim perforated paper to one square from stitching on all sides.

Tag Assembly

1. Cut a 6 x 3-inch piece from cardstock. Referring to photo, trim corners from one end to form tag.

2. Adhere cross-stitched ornaments to end of tag as shown.

3. Use pen to draw ornament "hangers" as shown. Hand-write "To:" and "From:" on tag.

4. Punch hole through left end of tag. Loop ribbon through hole; trim ends. ❖

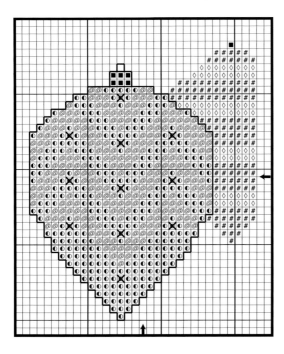

Ho! Ho! Ho! Stair-Step Card

Design by **Sharon Pope**

Materials
- 5 x 5-inch piece Wichelt Imports Inc. 14-count white perforated paper
- 1 skein each DMC 6-strand embroidery floss*
- Size 24 tapestry needle
- Stampin' Up! real red cardstock
- Scoring board and tool
- Craft knife
- Cutting mat
- Adhesive

*Refer to color code.

DMC®
·	blanc	white
■	321	red
◐	349	coral, dk.
ろ	350	coral, med.
@	351	coral
X	352	coral, lt.
♡	353	peach
☆	470	avocado green, lt.
○	747	sky blue, vy. lt.
/	758	terra cotta, vy. lt.
♥	825	blue, dk.
#	937	avocado green, med.
ℓ	3778	terra cotta, lt.
bs	310	black

Stitch Count
Santa: 42 x 42
Ho: 14 x 10 each (3)
Holly: 10 x 10 each (2)

Stitching Size
Santa: 3 x 3 inches
Ho: 1 x ¾ inch each (3)
Holly: ¾ x ¾ inch each (2)

Card Size
5½ x 4¼ inches

Stitching Instructions
1. Cross stitch over one square using two strands of floss.

2. Backstitch (bs) over one square using one strand 310.

3. Cut out stitched designs; trim perforated paper to one square from stitching on all sides of each piece.

Card Assembly

1. Cut a 5½ x 8½-inch piece from cardstock.

2. Place cardstock on cutting mat with short edge horizontal. Beginning 1 inch from top edge and 3 inches from right edge, use craft knife to cut a 5½-inch-long vertical line through cardstock (Photo 1).

Photo 3

Photo 4

scored lines on right side of card to create stair-step feature (Photo 4).

5. Referring to photo, adhere cross-stitched elements to the card. ❖

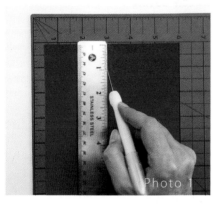

Photo 1

3. Rotate cardstock 90 degrees counterclockwise and place on scoring board. Use tool to score five vertical lines on top half of cardstock at 1-inch, 2-inch, 3¼-inch, 4½-inch and 6½-inch marks. Score one vertical line centered on bottom half of piece at 4¼-inch mark (Photo 2).

Photo 2

4. Fold center 4¼-inch line down to create card (Photo 3). Beginning with a mountain fold, accordion-fold card on the five horizontal

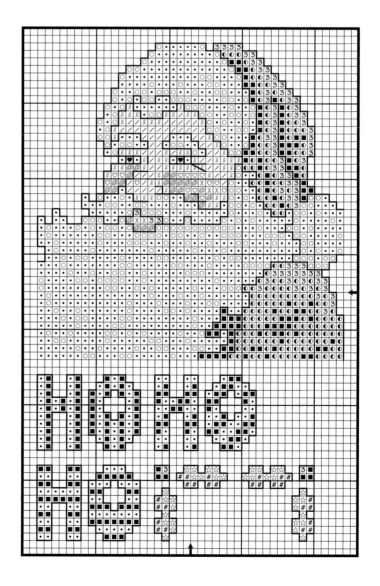

Winter Snow Globe Card

Design by **Elizabeth Spurlock**

Materials

- 5 x 5-inch piece Wichelt Imports Inc. 14-count white Aida
- 1 skein each DMC 6-strand embroidery floss*
- Size 24 tapestry needle
- Whimsiquills oval domed greeting card blank
- Stampin' Up! island indigo cardstock
- Starform silver text stickers (#310)
- Clear crystal beads
- Spellbinders™ Grand Ovals die templates (#LF-110)
- Die-cutting machine
- Adhesive

*Refer to color code.

DMC®

•	blanc	white
@	321	red
◗	469	avocado green
X	470	avocado green, lt.
○	518	Wedgwood, lt.
■	3799	pewter gray, vy. dk.

Stitch Count

34 x 34

Stitching Size

2⅜ x 2⅜ inches

Card Size

5¾ x 4⅛ inches

Stitching Instructions

1. Cross stitch over one square using two strands of floss.

2. Backstitch over one square using one strand 3799 for mouth, eyes and buttons; 321 for red portions of hat and for red scarf ends and fringe; 469 for remaining edges of scarf and hat (except for those portions of scarf adjacent to snowman's right shoulder); and 518 for all remaining backstitch.

3. Trim a 3¾ x 5⅛-inch rectangle around stitched image.

Card Assembly

1. Cut a 4¼ x 6-inch piece from blue cardstock.

2. Using smallest Grand Ovals die template, die-cut and emboss a 3¼ x 4¼-inch oval from center of blue rectangle. Adhere rectangle to front of card blank, centering card opening in cutout; trim edges even.

3. Adhere cross-stitched snowman to inside of card panel that will show through to card front.

4. Apply adhesive on front edges of clear dome; adhere to reverse side of card front, covering oval opening.

5. Fill clear dome with beads as desired. Apply adhesive along edges of dome and close card, sealing dome closed.

6. Attach sentiment and star stickers to card front as shown. ❖

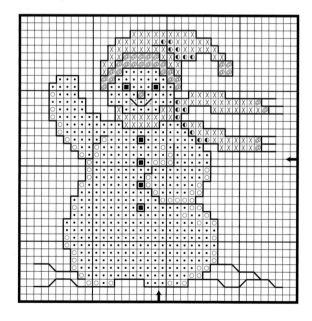

Holidays

LOVE Treat Bag Topper

Design by **Christy Schmitz**

Materials
- 4 x 4-inch piece Wichelt Imports Inc. 14-count antique brown perforated paper
- 1 skein each DMC 6-strand embroidery floss*
- Size 24 tapestry needle
- Stampin' Up! cardstock: pink pirouette, perfect plum
- Spellbinders™ Classic Scallop die templates (#E8-001)
- Die-cutting machine
- Scoring board and tool
- Adhesive

*Refer to color code.

DMC®
3	209	lavender, dk.
~	210	lavender, med.
◑	744	yellow, pl.
☆	745	pale yellow, lt.
£	954	Nile green
a	955	Nile green, lt.
○	963	dusty rose, ul. vy. lt.
@	3716	dusty rose, vy. lt.
bs	3801	melon, vy. dk.

Stitch Count
13 x 13 each (4)

Stitching Size
1 x 1 inch each

Bag Topper Size
6 x 2¼ inches

Stitching Instructions
1. Cross stitch over one square using two strands of floss and leaving at least two rows of empty squares between motifs.

2. Backstitch (bs) over one square using two strands 3801.

3. Cut out hearts, trimming perforated paper to one square from stitching on all edges of each piece.

Bag Topper Assembly
1. Cut a 6 x 4¼-inch piece from purple cardstock.

2. Using Edger die template with Scallop die insert, die-cut one long edge of purple cardstock.

3. Score and fold purple cardstock 1¾ inches from long straight edge to create bag topper base.

4. Cut a 6 x 1½-inch piece from pink cardstock; adhere to bag topper base as shown.

5. Adhere cross-stitched hearts to bag topper as shown. ❖

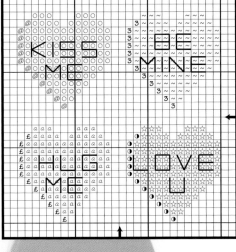

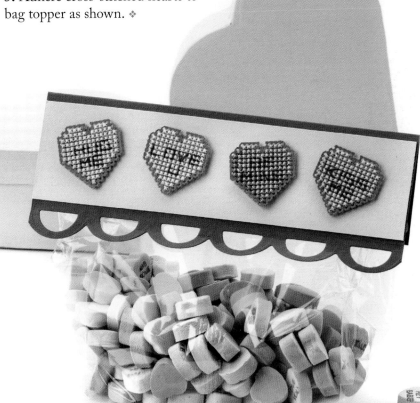

St. Patrick's Day Pin

Design by **Elizabeth Spurlock**

Materials
- 5 x 4-inch piece Wichelt Imports Inc. 14-count black Aida
- 1 skein each DMC 6-strand embroidery floss*
- Size 24 tapestry needle
- Stampin' Up! old olive cardstock
- Olive felt
- Pin back
- Adhesives: fabric glue, craft cement

*Refer to color code.

DMC®
¶	208	lavender, vy. dk.
@	322	baby blue, vy. dk.
♥	349	coral, dk.
ℓ	704	chartreuse, bt.
·	725	topaz, med. lt.
○	740	tangerine
■	792	cornflower blue, dk.
◑	909	emerald green, vy. dk.
X	911	emerald green, med.

Stitch Count
33 x 26

Stitching Size
2⅜ x 1⅞ inches

Pin Size
2⅞ x 2¼ inches

Stitching Instructions

1. Cross stitch over one square using two strands of floss.

2. Backstitch over one square using one strand 725 for veins in shamrock leaves and 909 to outline shamrock.

3. Trim a rectangle around design, trimming fabric to one square from widest point of stitching on all sides. Then trim design closely as shown from top left edge of rainbow to bottom of shamrock petal, trimming to one square from stitching along those edges.

Pin Assembly

1. Cut a 2⅞ x 2¼-inch rectangle from cardstock and a matching rectangle from felt; using fabric glue, adhere felt to cardstock to form pin base.

2. Center and adhere cross-stitched motif to felt side of pin base; use scissors to round off corners on left side as shown.

3. Using craft cement, adhere pin back to reverse side of pin. ❖

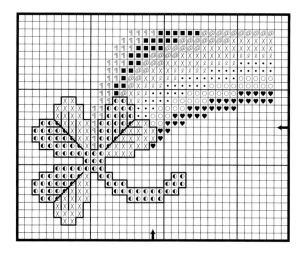

Materials

- 5 x 4-inch piece Wichelt Imports Inc. 14-count white perforated paper
- 1 skein each DMC 6-strand embroidery floss*
- Size 24 tapestry needle
- Stampin' Up! pink pirouette cardstock
- Black fine-tip pen
- 11 inches Gina K. Designs ⅝-inch pink sheer ribbon
- ⅛-inch hole punch
- Adhesive

*Refer to color code.

Easter Basket Tag

Design by **Breanne Jackson**

DMC®

◐	445	lemon, lt.
•	955	Nile green, lt.
♡	963	dusty rose, ul. vy. lt.
X	3761	sky blue, lt.
☆	3841	baby blue, pl.

Stitch Count
24 x 31

Stitching Size
1¾ x 2¼ inches

Tag Size
2⅜ x 3¾ inches

Stitching Instructions

1. Cross stitch over one square using two strands of floss.

2. Trim perforated paper to one square from stitching along all edges.

Tag Assembly

1. Cut a 2⅜ x 3¾-inch piece from cardstock. Trim top corners diagonally as shown to form tag base.

2. Adhere cross-stitched egg to tag.

3. Use pen to personalize tag.

4. Punch a hole in top of tag; loop ribbon through hole and trim ends. ❖

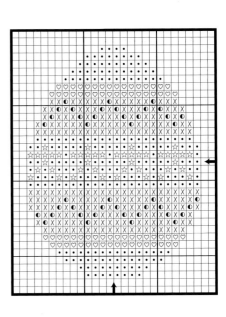

Flag Cupcake Topper

Design by **Elizabeth Spurlock**

Materials
- 5 x 5-inch piece Wichelt Imports Inc. 14-count white perforated paper
- 1 skein each DMC 6-strand embroidery floss*
- Size 24 tapestry needle
- Stampin' Up! cardstock: whisper white, real red, night of navy
- Lollipop stick
- Spellbinders™ Standard Circles LG die templates (#S4-114)
- Die-cutting machine
- Adhesive

*Refer to color code.

DMC®
•	blanc	white
@	321	red
○	322	baby blue, vy. dk.
~	728	topaz
/	775	baby blue, vy. lt.
☆	783	topaz, med.
■	803	baby blue, ul. vy. dk.
◑	815	garnet, med.

Stitch Count
33 x 33

Stitching Size
2⅜ x 2⅜ inches

Topper Size
2¾ inches in diameter

Stitching Instructions

1. Cross stitch over one square using two strands of floss.

2. Trim perforated paper to one square from stitching along all edges.

Cupcake Topper Assembly

1. Adhere cross-stitched image to white cardstock; trim, leaving a narrow border.

2. Use Standard Circles LG die templates to die-cut a 2⅜-inch circle from red cardstock and a 2¾-inch circle from navy cardstock.

3. Referring to photo, center and adhere red circle to navy circle; adhere cross-stitched flag to layered circles. Adhere topper to end of lollipop stick. ❖

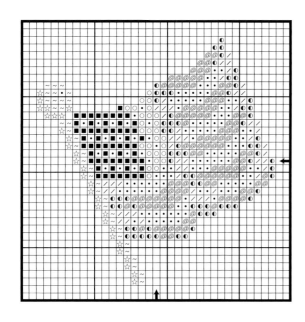

Materials

- 5 x 5-inch piece Wichelt Imports Inc. 14-count antique brown perforated paper
- 1 skein each DMC 6-strand embroidery floss*
- Size 24 tapestry needle
- Stampin' Up! cardstock: tangerine tango, crumb cake
- Gold fine-tip pen
- Scoring board and tool
- Adhesive

*Refer to color code.

Thanksgiving Place Card

Design by **Sharon Pope**

DMC®

■	355	terra cotta, dk.
@	434	brown, lt.
ℓ	435	brown, vy. lt.
•	738	tan, vy. lt.
X	976	golden brown, med.
~	977	golden brown, lt.
○	3830	terra cotta
bs	310	black

Stitch Count

34 x 23

Stitching Size

2³⁄₁₆ x 1⁵⁄₈ inches

Place Card Size

4 x 1⅞ inches

Stitching Instructions

1. Cross stitch over one square using two strands of floss.

2. Backstitch (bs) over one square using one strand 310.

3. Trim perforated paper to one square from stitching on each edge.

Place Card Assembly

1. Cut a 4 x 3-inch piece from dark orange cardstock; score and fold in half to form a 4 x 1½-inch place card.

2. Adhere cross-stitched piece to brown cardstock; trim edges even. Adhere to place card as shown.

3. Use gold pen to add name and decorative border. ❖

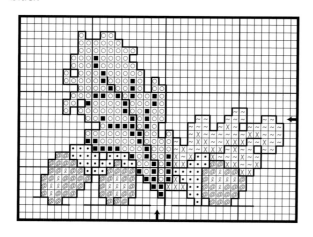

Materials

- 5 x 5-inch piece Wichelt Imports Inc. 14-count white Aida
- 1 skein each DMC 6-strand embroidery floss*
- Size 24 tapestry needle
- Stampin' Up! cardstock: tempting turquoise, Pacific point, whisper white
- Scoring board and tool
- Adhesive

*Refer to color code.

Hanukkah Gift Card

Design by **Christy Schmitz**

DMC®

X	blanc	white
■	434	brown, lt.
○	742	tangerine, lt.
@	825	blue, dk.
bs	640	beige gray, vy. dk.

Stitch Count
26 x 28

Stitching Size
2 x 2⅛ inches

Card Size
3⅛ x 3 inches

Stitching Instructions

1. Cross stitch over one square using two strands of floss.

2. Backstitch (bs) over one square using two strands 742 for candle flames and two strands 640 for candles.

3. Work straight stitch for star using two strands 825.

4. Cut a rectangle around stitched image, trimming fabric to one square from widest stitching along each edge.

Card Assembly

1. Cut a 3 x 6¼-inch piece from dark blue cardstock; score and fold in half to form a 3 x 3⅛-inch card base.

2. Adhere cross-stitched motif to turquoise cardstock and trim, leaving a narrow border. Adhere panel to white cardstock and trim, leaving a narrow border.

3. Adhere cross-stitched panel to card base as shown. ❖

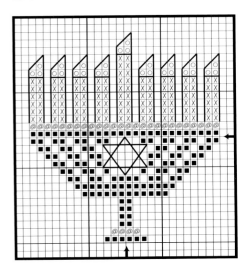

Buyer's Guide

The DMC Corp.
(973) 589-0606
www.dmc-usa.com

Elmer's® Products Inc.
(888) 435-6377
www.elmers.com

Gina K. Designs
(608) 838-3258
www.ginakdesigns.com

My Favorite Things
(352) 602-4071
www.mftstamps.com

Ranger Industries Inc.
(732) 389-3535
www.rangerink.com

Spellbinders™ Paper Arts
(888) 547-0400
www.spellbinderspaperarts.com

Stampin' Up!
(800) STAMP UP (782-6787)
www.stampinup.com

Starform
www.starform.com

We R Memory Keepers
(877) PICKWER (742-5937)
www.weronthenet.com

Whimsiquills
(877) 488-0894
www.whimsiquills.com

Wichelt Imports Inc.
(800) 356-9516
www.wichelt.com

The Buyer's Guide listings are provided as a service to our readers and should not be considered an endorsement from this publication.

Special Thanks to Our Model Stitchers

Cindy Herman
Happy Birthday Tag, page 7
BABY Gift Tag, page 13
Thank You Card, page 26
Thank You So Much, page 28
Holiday Ornaments Gift Tag, page 43

Michelle Munger
Celebrate!, page 10
Wedding Cake Tag, page 19
Thank You Tag, page 25
Lilies Sympathy Card, page 34
Candy Corn Tag, page 37
Boo! Swing Card, page 38
Hey Punkin!, page 40
LOVE Treat Bag Topper, page 49
Easter Basket Tag, page 51
Hanukkah Gift Card, page 54

Wava Rowe
Birthday Balloons Shaker Card, page 8
Elegant Gatefold Card, page 20
Get Well Easel Card, page 32
Winter Snow Globe Card, page 46
Thanksgiving Place Card, page 53

Ann Schmitz
Just Ducky Rocker Card, page 14
Boo! Swing Card, page 38
Ho! Ho! Ho! Stair-Step Card, page 44

Marcia Van Gelder
Welcome Little One, page 16
For the Love Birds, page 22
Forget-Me-Not Tag, page 31
St. Patrick's Day Pin, page 50
Flag Cupcake Topper, page 52

Annie's® *Easy Cross-Stitch Cards & Tags* is published by Annie's, 306 East Parr Road, Berne, IN 46711. Printed in USA. Copyright © 2014 Annie's. All rights reserved. This publication may not be reproduced in part or in whole without written permission from the publisher.

RETAIL STORES: If you would like to carry this pattern book or any other Annie's publication, visit AnniesWSL.com.

Every effort has been made to ensure that the instructions in this pattern book are complete and accurate. We cannot, however, take responsibility for human error, typographical mistakes or variations in individual work. Please visit AnniesCustomerCare.com to check for pattern updates.

ISBN: 978-1-57367-373-0
1 2 3 4 5 6 7 8 9